Speak,
Beautiful

Karen C. Elstub

Onwards and Upwards Publishers

Berkeley House, 11 Nightingale Crescent, Leatherhead,
Surrey, KT24 6PD.
www.onwardsandupwards.org

ISBN: 978-1-907509-73-5
Typeface: Sabon LT
Graphic design: Leah-Maarit

Endorsements

I smiled on the inside and the outside as I read 'Speak, beautiful' because Karen understands the unique struggle of women: to know and accept ourselves as beautiful. She has taken a journey into the heart of a man, into the heart of God: Jesus. There she has found the one thing that matters – to know herself as the Beloved. Whilst reading, I felt drenched in God's loving Word. I want to stick pages of this book all around my house. This book is truth and light for my fragile heart.

Fiona Mansford
Pure in Heart
March 2013

Dear Loved one,

You're blessed and highly favoured. Enjoy this book!

Love Karen x

13·5-13

About the Author

For over eighteen years, Karen Elstub has dedicated her time to teaching Music and English to secondary school students across south west London. Having been born again in 2002, her dream was to become a full time student and teacher of the Word of God. This dream finally came to pass in 2012; the fruit of a year's Bible study is *Speak, Beautiful.*

Contents

This book is dedicated to my
Heavenly Father, my Prince of
Peace and my Teacher.

Acknowledgements

I would like to thank my Heavenly Father for His watchful gaze over my life; thank You for sending Jesus to rescue me, and thank You for the gift of the Holy Spirit. He is a great best friend.

Thanks also to Bishop T D Jakes. I have sat under your teaching and anointing for the past ten years; you have changed my life. Get ready; get ready; get ready! The best is yet to come, Bishop!

And thank you to Serena, my beautiful daughter. What a privilege it is to be your Mum.

Karen C. Elstub
February 2013

Speak, Beautiful

Preface

The purpose of this book is to encourage you to become the beautiful woman you desire to be by simply changing what you speak. You see, everything around you has come about by words; nothing is unsaid. Someone has spoken out an idea which has, through a process of time, become visible on the earth. God created the world that we see by speaking it into existence (Genesis 1) and then He made us in His image (Genesis 1:26) expecting that we would do the same. When we speak things that are not yet visible out into the air, over a process of time they will become visible. This is true whether speaking positively or negatively. Words can create, change or reinforce a situation.

Like you, I have had to deal with many difficult situations, whether as a result of my own ignorance or the betrayal of loved ones. I have experienced the pain of being rejected, not knowing or understanding the reasons why. Consumed by grief and self-pity, I missed out on the freedom that only His truth can bring: that I am beautiful because He created me. By turning to Him in those darkest, heart-wrenching moments, I came to understand that my beauty and worth are not dependent on the acknowledgment of others but on His approval alone. It is great when people love you for who you are, but people come and go; your identity, worth and value need to be rooted in Him, the anchor of your soul, whose opinion of you will never change. When you discover that truth, ladies, you're free!

This book contains a lot of scripture. The Word of God is the only word that will empower you to become... you: the person you were created to be. You will no longer have to swim against the tide of social conformity; nor will you drown in the sea of confusion. You will be able to stay still and bloom where you're planted. His Word is that good and that powerful.

The *Beauty Secret* sections are little snippets, little reminders of truth. The *Notes* sections are for you to write down whatever you fancy. You could use it as a log, noting down any changes you notice as you meditate on the scripture.

Music is a great companion; listen to music that relaxes you as you meditate on the scriptures. Choose one or two Bible verses and really think about them. Give them time to enter your mind and spend the days ahead remembering their truth. When you're getting dressed for work or getting ready for bed, think on His Word. Remember what He says about you, and allow only this to be your truth. Get it in your mind, speak it out with your mouth and it will remain in your heart.

Sometimes the scriptures are paraphrased to allow the truth to be more personal. For example, Jeremiah 1:5 says, *"Before I formed thee in the belly I knew thee..."* but I have paraphrased it to read as *"He made me to be me. He loves me as I am because He has made me."*

I am sure there are a few of you out there that may be wondering, "How can I know for sure that God is talking to me here?" The answer is found in 2 Timothy:

> 2 Timothy 3:15-17 (The Message)
> *There's nothing like the written Word of God for showing you the way to salvation through faith in Christ Jesus. Every part of Scripture is God-breathed and useful one way or another— showing us truth, exposing our rebellion, correcting our mistakes, training us to live God's way. Through the Word we are put together and shaped up for the tasks God has for us.*

Be confident that the Bible was written with you in mind. You will find out who you are and who He is when you spend time in it.

Finally, put His Word in your mouth every day. It's not enough to just read it; you have to speak it. Put your name wherever it says 'I'. Thank Him for making you unique. Thank Him for who you are. As you begin to speak these words of beauty over yourself, you will become what you speak: beautiful.

INTRODUCTION

A Very Happy Beginning

---

*In the beginning, God created
the heavens and the earth.*

Genesis 1:1

I have noticed that the gap between what society calls beautiful and what I look like is becoming bigger and bigger. Keen to address all that's wrong with me, I plough through the latest fashion magazines, watch hours of popular TV programmes and the latest films in the hope of beholding a woman I could become in order to 'get that man' – or at least look beautiful enough to be wanted. But it never happens. The beauty eludes me.

> **Beauty Secret**
> The issue is not that there's something wrong with us; the issue is we don't know our true value (Hosea 4:6).

I can change my hairstyle, make up, clothes – even my body shape – but I still won't become a celebrated celluloid beauty. I still won't have that aura of celebrity. Do you know why? This beauty is a myth, a product of someone's imagination. Over the years, marketing executives have created ideas of what their woman needs to look/act/smell like in order to match the 'high quality' of the brand and therefore sell the product; and whether we realise it or not, those images have become our definition of feminine beauty. We can look at the images, then look at ourselves and realise the two just don't add up, leaving us to draw the conclusion that, "There must be something wrong with me."

When we compare ourselves to other women, we will either see ourselves coming up short (self-condemnation) or will think we are better than them (pride). When we are in these states, the voice of condemnation rears its ugly head and focuses our attention on how we feel: "I'm not pretty enough" or "I'm too attractive; men just want me for my looks and not for my heart".

It has only been through the deliberate study of God's word that I have realised that my worth and value as a woman goes beyond my curves and the magic of make-up. I have come to understand that beauty is on the outside and on the inside too. I have found out that God loves me but also *likes* me and will always like me because He wants to enjoy fellowship with me.

And this is your truth too.

This book has been written to let you know that **you are beautiful and deeply loved.**

NOTES

Beauty Secret
Look in the Word of God to see who you really are.

NOTES

CHAPTER ONE

Am I Beautiful?

The king is enthralled by your beauty; honour Him,
for He is your Lord.

Psalm 45:11

QUESTION: What is a girl to do when the word 'beauty' is constantly being redefined? How will she know that she is beautiful when change happens constantly?

ANSWER: She is to turn to the Good Book that will tell her, unequivocally, that she is beautiful because God says so and His word is true!

> ### Beauty Secret
> You are God's chosen
> dwelling place.
> 1 Corinthians 6:19

Think of all the women of faith who sought and found their identity in the spoken or written Word of God: Ruth, Rahab, Deborah, Sarah, Mary... What is more attractive and alluring than a woman who knows who she is in Jesus and rests in the truth that He loves her for who she is? Throughout your life you will hear so many differing opinions about you by others who know you well or not at all; it is important therefore to feed on God's word and allow only this to shape your character and define your worth; otherwise you'll be left out to sea.

God created us so that He could be in a relationship with us. He has chosen us as the object of His affection. God is a spirit and He fellowships with us through our spirit. In the Old Testament, the only way God's people could fellowship with Him was by entering His tabernacle or temple, even though only the priests could enter this place. King Solomon built God a magnificent temple in order to house the magnificent God. In this temple God promised to permanently be with the Israelites and never leave them. Solomon spared no expense with the temple. It was ornate, lavish, reverent, filled with precious stones and metals. He used the best materials available for God. Cross over into the New Testament and we find out that as believers in Jesus, God has chosen to make us His temple (1 Corinthians 6:19). Think about that for a moment. God has invested Himself... in you. You have been chosen. You are valuable to Him. He will always love you and will never leave you. Isn't that exciting?

Solomon's temple would have made God very happy. The commitment it took to complete it would have been no small thing. It was a visible statement of the goodness and magnitude of God. And yet, what pleases God even more than this is to have His people know Him, love Him and have Him dwelling within them. The care and attention Solomon gave to the building of the temple is nothing compared to how God cares for us. Your value, my value, resonates in the truth that we have been chosen. We are God's beautiful temple.

You may not feel beautiful, but it's time to stop living by your feelings and start living by the Word of God. It doesn't matter if you don't think that you are beautiful. If God says you are, you are. Receive through faith His beautiful description of you through His Word. It will change your life.

I Am Beautiful

He made me to be me. He loves me as I am because He has made me.
Jeremiah 1:5   *NLT*

I am precious and honoured in His sight.
Isaiah 43:4a   *NIV*

My feet are beautiful.
Song of Solomon 7:1a   *NLT*

My cheeks are lovely.
Song of Solomon 1:10   *NLT*

My mouth is lovely.
Song of Solomon 4:3   *NIV*

My hair is like a royal tapestry.
Song of Solomon 7:5   *NIV*

My hips are like jewels.
Song of Solomon 7:1   *NASB*

He calls me beautiful.
Song of Solomon 7:6   *NASB*

He desires me.
Song of Solomon 7:10   *NASB*

He loves the sound of my voice.
Song of Solomon 2:14   *NIV*

I have a garment of praise instead of a spirit of despair.
Isaiah 61:3   *NIV*

I am rooted and established in His love.
Ephesians 3:17   *NIV*

NOTES

CHAPTER TWO

Who Am I?

I am my Beloved's and He is mine.

Song of Solomon 6:3

I remember finding out for the first time that I would never truly know what I looked like; I could only rely on a reflection from a looking glass. It totally freaked me out! I wanted to pluck out my eyes, hold them in front of myself and take a good look at me. Thank goodness I never did! It's also true that whenever we look in a mirror or see a photo of ourselves, we not only *see* what we look like but we also *hear* what we look like. We might hear kind words from a loving friend or the affirming words of a lover or, sadly, our own voice telling us how terrible we look. In order to *see* who we really are, we must first *know* who we really are, and we can only know this truth by knowing what God says about us.

> **Beauty Secret**
> Use the mirror of God's word to find out who you are.

There is a problem with how we perceive ourselves, and this problem is called sin. When Adam disobeyed God, pride and self-righteousness replaced the identity and love we had in God. Mankind became uncomfortable, dis-eased with who they were, because they knew that through disobedience they had displeased God. The more mankind thought about sin, the worse they felt.

The gulf between God and man, caused by sin, was too great for man to both bear and restore. God took it upon Himself to restore man back to Himself through the sacrificial life of Jesus. Jesus' only purpose when He came to this earth was to unite us back to the Father which He achieved through His death on the cross. By believing in Him, you

> **Beauty Secret**
> Sin causes an internal war; belief in Jesus brings inner peace.

have been completely returned to God. And now, as born again believers in Christ, we have to find out through the word of God who we really are. When you continually hear God speaking His truth over you, your fractured soul finds peace and inner healing. Listening to and believing in the truth will not come easily because you are engaged in a battle between God and His enemy – and you are the reason why there is a war on!

The real war is not against other women beating you to being called 'the best-looking woman' or 'the most successful woman' or 'the woman who has got the best-looking husband'. *The real war is about your value.* Your enemy wants you to believe his lies that you are a worthless, good-for-nothing failure of a woman, and so he bombards your mind with these thoughts and supplies the 'evidence' with pictures of 'perfect' women. Satan wants to compare you in order to destroy you; God wants to focus on your uniqueness to celebrate you (Psalm 139:14). Satan's lies are designed to make us doubt our value and God's love for us (John 3:16) so that we will doubt God. These lies produce something very destructive in us. It is called condemnation.

> ## Beauty Secret
> Condemnation kills the very beauty and essence of who you are.

Condemnation means to blame, to hold responsible. It is a feeling that is overwhelming; *it kills the very beauty and essence of who you are.* Condemnation is not God's will for our lives; it does not come from God. It comes from Satan, our adversary.

In order to win a battle, you have to know your enemy. The one who hates us also hates God, which tells me that I'm on the same side as God – which is good news!

Seven truths you should know about the enemy

One His name is Satan; also known as the devil, Lucifer, the enemy. The Bible calls him 'Satan, the accuser of God's children' (Revelation 12:10b). He accuses us against God all the time, but when you're in Jesus, those accusations are lies and therefore cannot stand. Satan is defeated by the blood of the Lamb and by the word of our testimony (Revelation 12:11).

Two Satan wanted to be God but was unable to because there is only one true God. He rebelled against God and was cast out of heaven and into the earth (Revelation 12:9).

Three Satan is a created being (John 1:3). God created him as an angel (you can read a vivid description of what Satan looked like when God created him in Ezekiel 28:12-19). He wasn't created on the earth like man, which explains why we cannot see him; he was created in the heavens along with the rest of the angels whom we cannot see with our natural eyes.

Four He was beautiful but became prideful (Isaiah 14:13-14; Ezekiel 28:12-19). When he was cast out, a troop of angels went with him to set out to hurt God, knowing that he could never destroy him as he was an unequal match. How do you destroy an all-powerful God? By going after His heart – His creation – His people.

Five He hates the beauty of creation for he is no longer a part of it; he especially hates women because we played our role in bringing Jesus into this world (Genesis 3:15).

Six He has been defeated and is now under our feet! (Romans 16:20).

Seven The blood of Jesus destroys Satan's power (Hebrews 2:14 NLT).

Reject Satan's lies by speaking God's truth (His righteousness) over you. This will seem foreign when you first begin. After all, you're comfortable with those words that tell you you're inadequate, that things will go wrong because they always do. But stick with it! Decide that you will embrace *all* of God's word as truth and not just the parts

> **Beauty Secret**
> Hear the voice of righteousness and not condemnation.

you are comfortable with. For example, you might be happy to believe that you are His princess (Psalm 45:10-14), but you could have a big problem with Him being your loving Father (1 John 3:1). Do yourself a favour; *decide now to believe every good thing His Word says about you.* Hear His voice of righteousness speak life over you. Keep reading it and confessing it (speaking it out loud) until it becomes true to you (Romans 10:17; 12:1). Then one day you will look in your mirror (the Bible) and you'll love who

> **Beauty Secret**
> Know the one who knows you

you are; one day you will look in the mirror (looking glass) and you'll embrace who you see. One day you will know Him and therefore believe His Word.

This is who I am

I am the righteousness of God in Christ.
2 Corinthians 5:21   *NIV*

I am led on the path of righteousness because I bear His name.
Psalm 23:3   *NIV*

I am anointed with the oil of gladness.

Psalm 45:7   *ESV*

There is no condemnation in me.
Romans 8:1   *NIV*

I am free because the Holy Spirit lives in me...
1 Corinthians 6:19   *NIV*

...and where He is, there is freedom!
2 Corinthians 3:17   *NIV*

I am clothed in strength and honour.
Proverbs 31:25   *KJV*

I am created to solve a problem.
Genesis 2:18   *NLT*

I am made in His image.
Genesis 1:26   *KJV*

I am His bride.
2 Corinthians 11:2   *NLT*

I am His glorious inheritance.
Ephesians 1:18   *NLT*

I am more than a conqueror.
Romans 8:37   *NIV*

I am an overcomer of those things that would seek to destroy me.
Revelation 12:11   *KJV*

I am holy and blameless in sight – always...
Colossians 1:22   *NIV*

His blood speaks forgiveness over my life.
Hebrews 12:24   *NLT*

I am a well-watered garden, a fountain of unfailing water.
Isaiah 58:11   *DRB*

I am redeemed.
Revelation 5:9   *NIV*

I am highly favoured.
Luke 1:28   *NIV*

I am loved and cared for without the need to worry about anything.
Matthew 6: 25-26   *NIV*

I am a new creation in Him; the old has gone and the new has come.
2 Corinthians 5:17   *NIV*

I am His and He is mine.
Song of Solomon 6:3   *NIV*

NOTES

CHAPTER THREE

Who is Jesus?

Jesus is my resting place...

Matthew 11:28

...the Word made flesh.

John 1:14

The text book answer to the question 'Who is Jesus?' is to say that Jesus is the Son of God... but what does that mean to a woman who is wearied from a struggle to believe in a God whom she cannot see and touch, when the circumstances in her life are overwhelming?

> **Beauty Secret**
> When life overwhelms you, go and rest in the arms of Jesus, through His Word.

You only have to look at the women that came across Jesus' path to know how He would respond to you. When you take the Bible as truth, it is easier to settle in your mind what it has to say. Jesus loved women; that is undeniable. He saw a worth and value in them that society refused to acknowledge. He saw them as women and as individuals; he embraced their femininity and saw them as people, not objects. My favourite story in the Bible concerning Jesus and women is in Luke 7:11-16:

> *Soon afterward, Jesus went to a town called Nain, and his disciples and a large crowd went along with him. As he approached the town gate, a dead person was being carried out—the only son of his mother, and she was a widow. And a large crowd from the town was with her.*

Wow! Can you imagine this scene for just one moment? This woman is a widow – she has no husband to support her at this difficult time. Maybe he recently died. And now she is burying her only child – a son too, which would have been her only source of income. It's not right for a parent to be burying a child, and for her to be doing this on her own must have brought her immense pain. I can imagine the large crowd that was with her... I'm sure a lot of them were just there to watch – the kind of people that enjoy seeing other people suffer because it makes their pain easier to bear. Then there would have been the kind of people who went because they wanted to support her but were also interested in being part of a large community gathering. Maybe she was well known in the town. This was probably the worse day of her life as she was about to bury her son and her future too... and then came Jesus – my hero! Look at His reaction:

> *When the Lord saw her, his heart went out to her and he said, "Don't cry."*

Isn't that wonderful? He looked at her *and saw her*. He identified with her pain, her sense of loss, her hopelessness. In the book of Isaiah, Jesus is described as 'a man of sorrows' who took on our pains so that we could live a life of freedom in Him. What a wonderful promise we have in Him! Jesus, seeing and understanding the woman's plight, did something about it without her even asking Him too. In that moment, He met a widow and she encountered Grace. Maybe she didn't recognise Him or was caught up in grief and thought it was too late – but Jesus didn't think so. He was glad to have been there at the right time. Look what He does next:

> *Then he went up and touched the bier they were carrying him on, and the bearers stood still. He said, "Young man, I say to you, get up!"*

This is the Jesus I love and serve! He knew the crowds were watching. The widow had her crowd and Jesus had His. The atmosphere must have been a mixture of grief and tension when He spoke those words – not exactly an atmosphere of faith. Jesus took control of the situation; He took responsibility of the situation, despising the shame, humiliation and laughs from the scoffers that must have come when He spoke those faith-filled words. Jesus took the pressure off the widow and put it onto Himself, knowing that His faith would change her situation for the better. I love that! When we don't even have the mustard-seed-sized faith for an impossible situation, He is still there in control, making dead things come to life. The crowd would have been astonished with what happened next; even those following Jesus wouldn't have expected Him to raise a man from the dead who is lying in a coffin about to be buried. Maybe the widow wasn't even a follower of Jesus. Yet, His compassion for her caused Him to do the impossible. As a result,

> *The dead man sat up and began to talk, and Jesus gave him back to his mother.*

I can just imagine Jesus handing the son back; it would have had the grace and elegance of that moment when, at the end of a waltz, the gentleman holds out the lady's gloved hand and kisses it, thanking her for the dance. Jesus honoured the widow in that one moment, publicly restoring her hope, social standing, family relationships and financial security.

> *They were all filled with awe and praised God. "A great prophet has appeared among us," they said. "God has come to help his people."*

The widow's loss was an opportunity for God's restorative power sourced from a compassionate heart to come into play; she got her son back and God received the glory. Now the funeral can be remembered as the happiest day of her life!

So, who is Jesus? He is the Son of God, my resting place.

This is Christ Jesus

God is love.
1 John 4:8   NIV

He is responsible for taking care of me because I am His child; He is willing and able to fill my life with good things.
Matthew 7: 9-11   NIV

He has turned my mourning into dancing.
Psalm 30:11   KJV

He is the author and finisher of my faith.
Hebrews 12:2   KJV

He has the first word and final word in my life.
Revelation 21:6   NLT

He is the light of the world...
John 8:12   NIV

He has made me the light of the world.
Matthew 5:14   NIV

He is my healer.
Matthew 15:30   NLT

He is my lover.
Song of Solomon 7:10   NIV

He is my provision.
Philippians 4:19   NIV

He is my wisdom.
Luke 2:52; 1 Corinthians 2:16   NIV

He has told me to remain faithful to Him so that when I ask for anything, He will give it to me.
John 15:7   *NIV*

He has given me good things that pertain to life and godliness.
2 Peter 1:3   *NIV*

He has given me peace that surpasses all understanding; this peace reigns in my heart and mind.
Philippians 4:7   *NIV*

He has given me His mind.
Philippians 2:5   *ERV*

He does not condemn me...
John 3:17   *NIV*

...but instead reminds me of the righteousness I have in Him.
2 Corinthians 5:21   *NIV*

He is a God of increase.
2 Corinthians 9:10   *NLT*

He teaches me how to increase.
Luke 5:5   *NLT*

He makes everything beautiful in its time.
Ecclesiastes 3:11   *NIV*

He is my source of joy and life.
Romans 15:13   *NLT*

He is a good God...
Mark 10:18   *NIV*

...His mercy endures for ever.
Psalm 106:1   *NIV*

He pursues me with goodness and love.
Psalm 23:6   *NIV*

He has made all things, including me.
John 1:3   *NLT*

He is the word made flesh.
John 1:14   *NIV*

He is my hiding place and shield.
Psalm 119:114   *ESV*

He is my righteousness.
2 Corinthians 5:21   *NIV*

He is God with us.
Matthew 1:23   *NIV*

He is my burden carrier.
Matthew 11:28   *NIV*

He is my rest.
Matthew 11:28   *NIV*

NOTES

CHAPTER FOUR

What does Jesus Think about Me?

How beautiful and charming you are, my love, with your elegance.

Song of Solomon 7:6 (GWT)

We've just witnessed through the story of the widow of Nain that Jesus has a compassionate heart towards His people. He loves us. His love is consistent, valuable, long suffering, kind. It searches for us, finds us and then nurtures us back into wholeness and holiness for Him to enjoy. His love is a statement of who He is, not who we are. God is love (1 John 4:8). When we remember this truth, we realise that Jesus (who is the visible expression of God's love) doesn't think about us based on our deeds, our works. He thinks about us as His glorious creation, His children. When I know that I can't earn His love but I can receive and enjoy it, life takes on a different meaning. When we were children, we didn't (hopefully) try to do good things so that our parents would notice us and therefore be good to us; we just enjoyed playing in the sunshine or the rain or the snow, enjoying their expression of love towards us. That is the kind of life God wants for us. He wants us to enjoy Him just as He enjoys us.

To put it another way, Jesus is not thinking, "I wish she'd try harder; I wish she'd dress better; I wish she'd stop going out with that man." But He is thinking, "I love her so much. I made her to be this way and I love it! She is so beautiful! She is my daughter; my princess. Wow, I love her!" Get the picture? God loves you because He made you and not because of what you do. He just loves you!

> **Beauty Secret**
> God so loved ... me that He gave me His Son. (John 3:16)

Read the story of the widow of Nain again and ask yourself, what do you think Jesus thought of the widow? He wasn't physically present in her life, sharing the same spaces and faces, *yet He knew her* – isn't that our truth too?

God loved us while we were sinners, living life independently of Him. God loves us as His born again, spirit-filled children. He doesn't love us more because we're born again, and He didn't love us less as sinners. That's Grace! (2 Timothy 1:9) He loved the 'before Jesus' you and the 'after Jesus' you. If Heaven were to do a reality TV show with us, showing the change that happens to people when Jesus becomes their Lord, it wouldn't be called a 'makeover' show, it would be called a 'mind renewing' show (Romans 12:2). Not exactly catchy, I know. The Good News is, because Jesus has done away with sin (Hebrews 10:12), there is now nothing inadequate or wrong with us; we just need to line up our thoughts and words with His (Ephesians 4:23) so that the real, lasting, amazing change we desperately desire can take place in us.

God does not want to change you into a better person; He wants you to be connected to His unwavering love through His son so that you can become the person He has created you to be (Ephesians 2:10). You and I have everything we need to flourish as women of God: our hearts are the soil; His Word is the seed; His Love and Grace are the soil's nutrients; and His Holy Spirit is the water, revealing the truth of His Word. Now, go ahead and read His Word and blossom, you gorgeous lily! (Psalm 1:3; Song of Solomon 2:1)

What Christ Jesus thinks about me

I am the apple of His eye.
Deuteronomy 32:10   *NIV*

I am His princess.
Psalm 45:13   *NIV*

I am worthy of His love: He loves me so much, He died for me.
John 3:16   *NIV*

He sees me as His soldier.
Psalm 68:11   *NLT*

He sees more when He looks at me: I see a fisherman; He sees a fisher of men.
Luke 5:10   *NLT*

NOTES

NOTES

CHAPTER FIVE

What do I Mean to Him?

You are the apple of My eye.

Deuteronomy 32:10

God is our Creator and He is our Father; we are His children. It is impossible for loving parents to ignore or devalue their children. Love demands the best for others, and so it is impossible for God to love us as His children and not value us. We mean everything to Him; if it were not so, He wouldn't have sent Jesus into the world for us (John 3:16). It does take a renewing of the mind (Romans 12:2) to grasp what the love of God means to us. Some of us may have struggled with our earthly fathers not loving us as we would want or deserve, but it is important to meditate on who God says He is and to take Him at His Word rather than to understand Him from our limited experiences of earthly fatherly love.

So, the answer to the question is: yes, we mean everything to God. He does not need us to be God, but we need Him! He loves us and desires fellowship with us; He made us to enjoy us. He thought about us and created us before He created the world (Ephesians 1:4). He has put a lot of thought into who we are, what we would do here on earth and what we would need to accomplish it. The Holy Spirit, speaking through the apostle Paul, describes us as God's workmanship (Ephesians 2:10). The New Testament was written in Greek. The word *workmanship* was the Greek word *poemia* which means *poem* and *poetry* in English. Now think about that – you are a piece of poetry! Everything about you is rhythmical, lyrical. All poets will tell you that every word matters; no word is superfluous, an add-on because they couldn't think of anything else or they needed it to rhyme. Just as every word in a poem has a purpose in order to display the poet's intentions, everything about our lives combine with divine leading and purpose to create the perfect poem for the glory of God.

> **Beauty Secret**
> Remember that you are God's child whom He dearly loves.
> (1 John 3:2)

Read the poem *'Love (III)'* by George Herbert (1593 – 1633) to see how he succinctly describes God's love for His children. Imagine the time spent on choosing the right words so that the right message would be heard; imagine how true Herbert had to stay to himself in order to accurately represent what he was feeling. Imagine how words, rhythm, phrasing, punctuation all had a part to play in the creation of this poem. And then remember that you are God's own poem.

Love (III)

Love bade me welcome: yet my soul drew back,
Guilty of dust and sin.
But quick-eyed Love, observing me grow slack
From my first entrance in,
Drew nearer to me, sweetly questioning,
If I lacked any thing?

'A guest', I answered, 'worthy to be here':
Love said, 'You shall be he.'
'I the unkind, ungrateful? Ah, my dear
I cannot look on thee.'
Love took my hand, and smiling did reply,
'Who made the eyes but I?'

'Truth, Lord, but I have marred them: let my shame
Go where it doth deserve.'
'And know you not,' says Love, 'who bore the blame?'
'My dear, then I will serve.'
'You must sit down,' says Love, 'and taste my meat':
So I did sit and eat.

George Herbert

Ephesians 2:10 (GWT)
God has made us what we are. He has created us in Christ Jesus
to live lives filled with good works that he has prepared for us to
do.

NOTES

CHAPTER SIX

...And a Very Happy Ending

The Grace of our Lord Jesus Christ
be with you all. Amen.

Revelation 22:21

By the grace of God, we are called His children (John 1:12). When God looks at us, He doesn't see all the 'ugly', imperfect things that we see. He sees us as beautiful women who were made in His image (Genesis 1:27). He sees us as perfect and blameless because of Jesus (Ephesians 5:25-27). He sees us as a worthy investment of His Son's life. Our physical appearance is important as it is unique to us; but it will never represent our value and worth that our lives hold in Christ Jesus. When you know the truth of how much you mean to God, your fear of not being enough or the need to make and keep yourself beautiful will break off your life.

> **Beauty Secret**
> You are esteemed and valued by God

You may not have the body shape you want; you may not be married or have children; your hair may not be straight enough or the right shade of blonde. But know this: you are esteemed and valued by God because you are His, and He calls you His beloved, the same word He used to describe His relationship with Jesus (Song of Solomon 6:3; Mark 9:7). Go on and shout hallelujah!

Speak over the lies with the truth of God's Word!

> **Beauty Secret**
> Choose one scripture a day and memorise it. Speak it over your life until you know it is true.

As born again, spirit-filled believers, we should see the Bible as our mirror and our identity. It gives us the complete picture as to what we should look like physically, mentally, emotionally and spiritually. It tells us who we are in Christ Jesus; it tells us who this Jesus is. When lies of condemnation start to speak to you, let your faith rise up and speak back to it – out loud – with what God's Word says about you.

God says to me that...

I am fearfully and wonderfully made.
Psalm 139:14   *NIV*

Before I was in my mother's womb, He called me and knew me...
Jeremiah 1:5   *NIV*

I am the head and not the tail...
Deuteronomy 28:13   *NIV*

...I am above and not beneath.
Deuteronomy 28:15   *KJV*

I am the lender and not the borrower.
Deuteronomy 28:13   *NIV*

I am seated in heaven in Christ Jesus.
Ephesians 2:6   *ABPE*

I am rooted and established in love.
Ephesians 3:17   *NIV*

There is no condemnation in me.
Romans 8:1   *NIV*

He loves me so much, He died for me.
John 3:16   *NIV*

He gives me the weapon of praise to defeat complacency, tiredness and hopelessness.
Isaiah 61:3   *NIV*

He will never allow me to beg for bread.
Psalm 37:25   *NIV*

I am a child of light.
1 Thessalonians 5:5   *NLT*

I am His righteousness.
2 Corinthians 5:21   *NIV*

I am forever loved.
Jeremiah 31:3   *NIV*

NOTES

Appendix: List of Scriptures

Bible Versions

ABPE	*Aramaic Bible in Plain English, 2010 edition*
DRB	*Douay-Rheims Bible*
ESV	*English Standard Version*
ERV	*English Revised Version*
KJV	*King James Version, Cambridge edition*
NASB	*New American Standard Bible*
NIV	*New International Version, 1984 edition*
NLT	*New Living Translation, 2007 edition*

Chapter One

He made me to be me. He loves me as I am because He has made me.
Jeremiah 1:5   *NLT*

I am precious and honoured in His sight.
Isaiah 43:4a   *NIV*

My feet are beautiful.
Song of Solomon 7:1a   *NLT*

My cheeks are lovely.
Song of Solomon 1:10   *NLT*

My mouth is lovely.
Song of Solomon 4:3   *NIV*

My hair is like a royal tapestry.
Song of Solomon 7:5   *NIV*

My hips are like jewels.
Song of Solomon 7:1   *NASB*

He calls me beautiful.
Song of Solomon 7:6   *NASB*

He desires me.
Song of Solomon 7:10   *NASB*

He loves the sound of my voice.
Song of Solomon 2:14   *NIV*

I have a garment of praise instead of a spirit of despair.
Isaiah 61:3   *NIV*

I am rooted and established in His love.
Ephesians 3:17   *NIV*

Chapter Two

I am the righteousness of God in Christ.
2 Corinthians 5:21   *NIV*

I am led on the path of righteousness because I bear His name.
Psalm 23:3   *NIV*

I am anointed with the oil of gladness.
Psalm 45:7   *ESV*

There is no condemnation in me.
Romans 8:1   *NIV*

I am free because the Holy Spirit lives in me...
1 Corinthians 6:19   *NIV*

...and where He is, there is freedom!
2 Corinthians 3:17   *NIV*

I am clothed in strength and honour.
Proverbs 31:25   *KJV*

I am created to solve a problem.
Genesis 2:18   *NLT*

I am made in His image.
Genesis 1:26   *KJV*

I am His bride.
2 Corinthians 11:2   *NLT*

I am His glorious inheritance.
Ephesians 1:18   *NLT*

I am more than a conqueror.
Romans 8:37   *NIV*

I am an overcomer of those things that would seek to destroy me.
Revelation 12:11   *KJV*

I am holy and blameless in sight – always...
Colossians 1:22   *NIV*

His blood speaks forgiveness over my life.
Hebrews 12:24   *NLT*

I am a well-watered garden, a fountain of unfailing water.
Isaiah 58:11   *DRB*

I am redeemed.
Revelation 5:9   *NIV*

I am highly favoured.
Luke 1:28   *NIV*

I am loved and cared for without the need to worry about anything.
Matthew 6: 25-26   *NIV*

I am a new creation in Him; the old has gone and the new has come.
2 Corinthians 5:17   *NIV*

I am His and He is mine.
Song of Solomon 6:3   *NIV*

Chapter Three

God is love.
1 John 4:8   *NIV*

He is responsible for taking care of me because I am His child; He is willing and able to fill my life with good things.
Matthew 7: 9-11   *NIV*

He has turned my mourning into dancing.
Psalm 30:11   *KJV*

He is the author and finisher of my faith.
Hebrews 12:2   *KJV*

He has the first word and final word in my life.
Revelation 21:6　　　　　　　*NLT*

He is the light of the world...
John 8:12　　　　　　　　*NIV*

He has made me the light of the world.
Matthew 5:14　　　　　　　*NIV*

He is my healer.
Matthew 15:30　　　　　　　*NLT*

He is my lover.
Song of Solomon 7:10　　　　*NIV*

He is my provision.
Philippians 4:19　　　　　　*NIV*

He is my wisdom.
Luke 2:52; 1 Corinthians 2:16　　*NIV*

He has told me to remain faithful to Him so that when I ask for anything, He will give it to me.
John 15:7　　　　　　　　*NIV*

He has given me good things that pertain to life and godliness.
2 Peter 1:3　　　　　　　*NIV*

He has given me peace that surpasses all understanding; this peace reigns in my heart and mind.
Philippians 4:7　　　　　　*NIV*

He has given me His mind.
Philippians 2:5　　　　　　*ERV*

He does not condemn me...
John 3:17　　　　　　　　*NIV*

...but instead reminds me of the righteousness I have in Him.
2 Corinthians 5:21　　　　　*NIV*

He is a God of increase.
2 Corinthians 9:10　　　　　*NLT*

He teaches me how to increase.
Luke 5:5　　　　　　　　*NLT*

He makes everything beautiful in its time.
Ecclesiastes 3:11   *NIV*

He is my source of joy and life.
Romans 15:13   *NLT*

He is a good God...
Mark 10:18   *NIV*

...His mercy endures for ever.
Psalm 106:1   *NIV*

He pursues me with goodness and love.
Psalm 23:6   *NIV*

He has made all things, including me.
John 1:3   *NLT*

He is the word made flesh.
John 1:14   *NIV*

He is my hiding place and shield.
Psalm 119:114   *ESV*

He is my righteousness.
2 Corinthians 5:21   *NIV*

He is God with us.
Matthew 1:23   *NIV*

He is my burden carrier.
Matthew 11:28   *NIV*

He is my rest.
Matthew 11:28   *NIV*

Chapter Four

I am the apple of His eye.
Deuteronomy 32:10   *NIV*

I am His princess.
Psalm 45:13   *NIV*

I am worthy of His love: He loves me so much, He died for me.
John 3:16   *NIV*

He sees me as His soldier.
Psalm 68:11   *NLT*

He sees more when He looks at me: I see a fisherman; He sees a fisher of men.
Luke 5:10   *NLT*

Chapter Six

I am fearfully and wonderfully made.
Psalm 139:14   *NIV*

Before I was in my mother's womb, He called me and knew me...
Jeremiah 1:5   *NIV*

I am the head and not the tail...
Deuteronomy 28:13   *NIV*

...I am above and not beneath.
Deuteronomy 28:15   *KJV*

I am the lender and not the borrower.
Deuteronomy 28:13   *NIV*

I am seated in heaven in Christ Jesus.
Ephesians 2:6   *ABPE*

I am rooted and established in love.
Ephesians 3:17   *NIV*

There is no condemnation in me.
Romans 8:1   *NIV*

He loves me so much, He died for me.
John 3:16   *NIV*

He gives me the weapon of praise to defeat complacency, tiredness and hopelessness.
Isaiah 61:3   *NIV*

He will never allow me to beg for bread.
Psalm 37:25   *NIV*

I am a child of light.
1 Thessalonians 5:5   *NLT*

I am forever loved.
Jeremiah 31:3   *NIV*

Prayer

If you don't know Jesus Christ as your Lord and Saviour, and would like to receive Him in your life, then pray this prayer:

Salvation Prayer

Lord Jesus, I believe that You are the Son of God. I believe that You died on the cross for me because You love me. I believe that You rose from the dead and that You are alive today.

I choose to make You my Lord and Saviour. Thank You for Your precious blood that washes me clean from every sin. Thank You that my life is now in You. I receive Your unconditional love and forgiveness. I now live to love You and know You more.

Amen.

Author's Website

For further information, please visit the author's website:

www.karenelstub.com